SEEDS OF LIGHT

Aphorisms of Swami Sivananda Radha

Swami Sivananda Radha is the founder and spiritual director of Yasodhara Ashram, a yoga retreat and study center located in Kootenay Bay, British Columbia, Canada. She is also the founder and president of the Association for the Development of Human Potential in the United States. She received her training at Sivananda Ashram in Rishikesh, India, and, at the request of her Guru, Swami Sivananda Saraswati, returned to the West in 1956 to help disseminate the yogic teachings and practices. Her major emphasis has been to interpret the ancient teachings so that they can be understood and applied in the daily lives of Westerners.

The concise messages presented in this book derive their powerful impact from the Kundalini Yoga system of spiritual growth, a direct path to higher consciousness. "Seeds of Light" serves as a companion volume to "Kundalini: Yoga for the West," Swami Radha's major presentation of the path of Kundalini Yoga. She writes with a depth of understanding and wisdom which reflects her own intensive practice of yoga in daily living for over thirty years. Special emphasis is given to the spiritual potential of women.

Other Books by The Author

Kundalini: Yoga for the West
Radha: Diary of a Woman's Search
Hatha Yoga: The Hidden Language
The Hatha Yoga Workbook
Mantras: Words of Power
The Divine Light Invocation

Available from:

Timeless Books
PO Box 50905
Palo Alto, CA 94303-0673
(415) 321-8311

In Canada
PO Box 9
Kootenay Bay, B.C. V0B 1X0
(604) 227-9224

Seeds
of
Light

Swami Sivananda Radha

Timeless Books

publishers of timeless wisdom

1991

TIMELESS BOOKS
PO Box 50905
Palo Alto, CA 94303-0673
(415) 321-8311
In Canada: Timeless Books, Box 9, Kootenay Bay, B.C. V0B 1X0 - (604) 227-9224
In England: Timeless Books, 7 Roper Rd., Canterbury, Kent CT2 7EH - (0227) 768813

Originally published as *Aphorisms of Swami Sivananda Radha* in 1980
First edition of *Seeds of Light* published 1985
Printed in the United States of America

Illustrations by Margaret White
Calligraphy by Deborah Pohorsky
Photo credits: front cover photo courtesy Reflexion
            back cover photo of Swami Sivananda Radha courtesy Derek French

Library of Congress Cataloging-in-Publication Data:
Sivananda Radha, Swami 1911-
        [Aphorisms of Swami Sivananda Radha]
        Seeds of light / Swami Sivananda Radha ; [illustrations by
        Margaret White].
        p. cm.
        previously published as: Aphorisms of Swami Sivananda Radha.
        ISBN 0-931454-22-0
        1. Hindu meditations I. White, Margaret, 1924-   . II. Title.
        [BL 1146.S56A6 1991]
        294.5' 43--dc20   90-49580
                                                       CIP

ISBN 0-931454-22-0

Key sentences are reminders in a nutshell.

Contents

Swami Radha

Introduction

Be set on awareness and that in itself will carry you in your growth.

"Seeds of Light" is a collection of Swami Radha's key sentences, or aphorisms, that succinctly capture the special magic of her teachings. Collected from her workshops and lectures over many years, these key sentences express the Teachings that she brought from the East, presenting them in terms that the Western mind can understand. In her special blend of inspiration and practicality she offers us the path to liberation from our limitations, our attachments, and our ego desires.

Swami Radha is like the good gardener who plants only the very best seeds: seeds of Light, seeds of wisdom. Each one of us has the power to choose what to plant in the garden of the mind: negative thoughts like thistles of self-importance and greed, or insights like roses that will blossom into inspiration and inner knowing. Swami Radha suggests using the tool of reflection to cultivate understanding and awareness.

This book offers many seed thoughts that we can apply in daily life, using our reflections to nurture them. I have used these aphorisms as reminders to change my own habitual ways of thinking, in order to refocus my mind constructively. I want to build a life of quality and awareness, and I can use my mind as a tool to help me do it.

In preparing for the drawings in this book, I began by quieting my mind, then turned my attention to the essence of one "saying in a nutshell." My reflection allowed questions to emerge, revealing my own discoveries and insights that led to the image of the drawing.

For example, I thought about the saying, "There is only one truth. There appear to be many truths because of different understandings." Questions arose: What is that one truth? How can I find it? How can I know it? What are the different understandings of it? I felt a longing for the one truth as a kind of thirst. I envisioned people searching for a source of pure clear water to assuage that thirst that sustains the spirit within. An image came to mind of many people bringing their various kinds of containers and vessels to the source to collect that water of truth. Further reflection led me to explore how we have distorted the one truth and used it selfishly.

There are many ways of using these Seeds of Light: take one each day to focus on, writing out the insights that arise; make several copies of a favorite aphorism and put them in strategic places for a week, noting your observations and discoveries; reflect on one before going to sleep, then observe your dreams.

May you gather a harvest of inspiration and practical guidance from your contact with this powerful little book.

Swami Durgananda
Kootenay Bay, B.C.

**Another person can only inspire you.
You grow by your own efforts.**

Identification

"I am not the body.
I am not the mind.
I am Light Eternal."

Identify first
with Light, then the essence of Light.

When chanting mantras you are slowly, gradually changing identification.

Never identify except with your Higher Self.

An image too often recalled, too long held, takes on a life of its own.

Use an image as a focal point only. If you identify with Jesus or Buddha you cannot be yourself. Look for your identity within. Identify with the Higher Self or inner Light. Anything else is pretending.

I cannot know you if I hold on to the image I have of you.

I can truly know you only when you reveal Yourself to me.

Cosmic Consciousness is beyond shape, beyond form, beyond name. Find out who you are beyond surface appearances.

Your dream lover is your Higher Self.

"I am functioning from the center."

You close the door to Liberation by slipping back into
identification with body, emotions and mind.

Your body
is a spiritual tool. Appreciate the miracle that it is.

Your true nature is incomprehensible to your intellect.

An act of surrender can only truly take place when your will
is no longer bound in self

Be yourself. Put assumptions away about what you
should be. These are a waste of time.

Mirror, mirror on the wall — what do I see? A face of pain?
A face of resentment? A face of hate? Or a face of
love and of kindness? What is my true reflection?

Reflect on what you have. If you don't like it, throw it out.
You don't have to analyze everything.

Put energy into a search for the higher values of life.
While eating identify with the energy in the food; while listening to
music identify with the vibration created by sound; during the sex
act identify with the union of the Higher Self of each partner.

6

Do not identify with other persons and their problems.
Be detached to be of help, as is the surgeon
who cuts out a cancer.

Your spiritual life must be very real. You must be real.

Don't assume that you should always be the same. That
is an impossibility.

You have a right to your own path. Don't compare yourself
to another. Comparison is judgement and competition.

Rather than identify with the Guru, look intentionally
for the Divine in the Guru.

The first step toward wholeness or 'hol·i·ness'
is self-discipline and self-control.

The sound of Om absorbs all images and forms,
as all colors are contained in white.

The image you have of God is His rival.

Dissolve images
**of yourself and images of God. Then God is
no longer a supreme being, but Power itself.**

Make yourself the temple of the Most High.

Personality Aspects

Who am I?

A personality? Which one and how many?
Personality is short lived. Self is eternal.

When you feel hurt, look at the personality aspect that is injured.

If you cannot hear the "still, small voice", the soul, or the "goddess within", it is because of the mental background noises caused by self-justification in defense of the ego.

The Higher Self

should be the ruler of our lives. Why give power and authority to personality aspects? They will only war with each other.

**Desire is an insatiable beast.
It never gets enough.**

If you have to forgive yourself for something, it can only be something you did intentionally against your better knowledge.

You cannot stop being a robot unless you know to what degree you are one.

Make the decision to speak only when it is important. Energy is wasted in talking.

Talking about the past only re-inforces it.

Don't give your opinions unless asked.

The ways of developing spirituality are through short intense periods of meditation; acceptance of your own divinity through use of the Divine Light Invocation; chanting mantra; practice of awareness and discrimination.

Hostility and resentment point to ego, to self-importance.

New attachments keep you going, keep you moving, keep you restless.

Needs come and go. Watch which ones you feed.

Do not trust your personality aspects. They are living on the input of your senses.

Overly modest statements come from a false, inverted ego.

The small "e" ego is vanity and pride. The large "E" Ego is a type of energy which holds the body together and keeps it functioning.

Shyness is inverted ego. You do not want to expose yourself to possible criticism.

Seek the good,
the positive, the creative. Then that is what you open yourself to and that is what you respond to.

Mistakes are not sins. Stop being critical of your own mistakes and the mistakes of others.

Let off steam at times if necessary, but don't make anyone the target.

Public confession is not necessary, it is not part of honesty. If the problem is too horrible to confess, write it down. Pour out your heart; reflect; pray for forgiveness; forgive others involved. Burn the paper. Leave it in God's hands and forget it.

Is punishment ever justified? Yes, if you can't remember, you must be reminded.

Dreams of death and dying mean the death of that particular
aspect of ego. We have a multitude of personalities,
each having its own ego.

If you were really humiliated, you had tremendous
attachment and blindness.

When you have a desire for revenge, what can you hurt
except all the personality aspects, each with its own ego.

Curb self-expression, self-centredness, selfishness,
self-gratification. All difficulties arise from these.

God is not an old man in heaven.
God is energy and Light.

The mind is a house. The Higher Self wants to take charge of the house and throw out the false ego and personality aspects. The personality aspects are parasites, living on your life force.

Human emotions
are the electricity on which the Divine Energy can travel.

If you are accused and react emotionally or with anger, understand that in some way, on some level, it is true.

Any place of life is a battlefield. Personality aspects are ghosts and they have no reality. Fight until they are recognized as a creation of your own mind.

Withdraw energy and power from personality aspects. Let it flow into positive or creative channels.

A magnifying glass has the purpose to enlarge. What? The negative or the positive? In whom?

Don't give attention or energy to unimportant habitual reactions, expressions or little mannerisms of people. Give the energy instead to spiritual practice.

You can train those aspects of yourself which need cultivation instead of criticising yourself for their lack.

Criticism is based on a firmly established value system.

The discovery of negative aspects and limitations in your self should not be seen as something evil. They are part of the perfection of life, one half of the unit. Without knowing the darkness of night, the light of day is not enjoyed.

The sun and shadow always go together. They both have to be accepted.

Life is not a straight line. We have to allow ourselves waves of ups and downs. My will gives the momentum to bring me back up again.

No two sounds have the same vibration, yet there can be harmony.

The Two Selves in me are One.

Freedom:
the acceptance of the rational and the irrational.
They are the roots of the same tree.

Especially for Women

True love

between man and woman is only possible when there is no emotional dependence. They can then become each other's best friend.

The major problem facing woman is to develop her emotional independence. She can do this by recognizing her Divine nature.

Woman's nature is to preserve. Her nurturing instincts should never be turned into a destructive force.

Woman should not allow the anger accompanying the womens' liberation movement to turn her against her nature.

The revolution of women can be a revelation, a liberation.

The female must develop maleness
in a fifty-fifty proportion.

The male must develop femaleness
in a fifty-fifty proportion.

Only women who can break loose from limiting attachments can find liberation in one lifetime.

It is difficult for women to change, one reason being the tenacity with which husbands and children hang on to the old image.

Are you grateful for perfect children? Now you want a perfect husband!

To come into their own women must establish their own values and bring up their children accordingly without attacking men.

You will be closer to the child with the same sense dominance.

Marriage and children are cultural ideas. A woman does not have to accept them.

Women should outgrow their baby shoes and stand on their own feet.

When women dare voice their true thoughts to themselves, they have the freedom to shift total devotion from husband and family to higher goals.

Without women's inspiration, man could do nothing.

It is women who seek quality and who are willing to accept other forces in life, such as intuition.

Woman has always
been interpreted by man. A psychology of women does not exist.

Equality of all — no. Equal opportunity — yes.

Independence is desired, but conformity prevails, sometimes only slightly disguised.

The strongest hold on most of us is emotional security, looking outside ourselves for that which can only be found within. There is no security that we can really find in another person.

Most people need approval, acceptance and appreciation from others. Dependence on these needs prevents us from being free to be ourselves and to develop our own talents.

Regarding abortion,
no single rule applies to everyone.

We murder all the time — plants, animals that we eat or walk on. Suppose a mountain falls down and we all die. Who murdered us? God? The life force is constantly being murdered. The last authority is our own conscience. If the mother refuses entrance to a soul, the soul has to find another place to go. The impact, the troublesome aspect, may not be as great as we think.

27

Divine Mother

worship is nothing more than accepting creation
in the smallest detail and in all people.

White Tara

Love

Love is listening;
your true concern is there. No one can ever truthfully say 'I love you' and then not listen.

When you listen you have to surrender criticism, otherwise you don't really listen. Listen with intuition.

Only when you can be friends and have consideration, only when you can love and listen will sexual union be a mystical experience.

Do I really love this person or do I love my image of this person? We all have an image of each other with expectations.

There is no mechanicalness in love or contentment.

Learn to listen
with your inner ear. It is sensitive to the
vibration of your voice.

Cultivate gratitude
and never be too shy to express it.

Without gratitude you will never receive more. That seems to be some kind of Divine Law.

The only obligation you have is to fulfill the purpose for which you have come into life. This obligation is to fulfill the Divine within and to share it with others.

Do God's work without ego, with a sense of selfless service. Do not be possessive or have expectations. You must let the ego go in order to truly be a channel.

Try to understand the other person in depth. Superficiality prevents closeness.

When sharing your experience or activities, consider your motivation and the possible effect on the other person. Sharing is not always caring.

The highest form of love has no "because" attached to it.

Doing the best thing you can for another out of love may not be pleasing to that person, may not be what is wanted, may not be accepted.

If someone says "I love you" too often, there is a need to convince himself.

Forgiveness is love manifest.

There is only one love, God's love.

Reasons for love?

**There can be no reasons. Either you love
or you don't love**

Possessive love is enslavement.

Have no ambition to help anyone more than they ask.

Be non-possessive in a relationship. Don't look for
security by attempting to own something
that is not yours.

If you can't feel love you can be considerate,
a true human being.

When love is experienced as an emotion, desire is still there
in the form of attachments and gratification. Emotion
refined into feeling can then raise you to a sense of the
power of love as a Divine force.

In the course of life there are many little "miracles" but our hearts are so hardened that we don't pay attention to them. Instead we take them for granted.

The plight of another is your opportunity to develop compassion to an almost Divine degree.

Compassion based in ignorance is cowardice, not peace-harmony.

It is wrong to take all the blame for negative happenings and no praise for good happenings. Acknowledge where you play your own part.

Selfless service is giving of oneself without asking for rewards.

Mercy is forgiveness, understanding coming from the heart.

Let God's light shine through your eyes.

Pain and Suffering

Pain is a great teacher.

Find out what the lesson is. When you have learned it, the body will heal itself.

By the power of suggestion you can manipulate
yourself into negative or positive behavior. You can invite pain.
Or you can program yourself to be well and happy.

You can tell yourself you can't do something, ensuring that
in due time you won't be able to.

Use the power of choice to minimize pain.

Look always in the mental when there is something manifesting
in the physical. It can be a signal of dissatisfaction
from the Higher Self.

Wake up
**from the dream of life when it is sad and depressing.
Wake up to another level of consciousness.**

Every time you grow in understanding you grow to a new level.
When a situation in life is painful, shift into a higher level.
The pain will lose its reality.

Understanding comes first. Surrender to what is understood
comes next.

Pain and joy — a pair of opposites. If you desire pleasure,
you experience pain. The path of Yoga means going beyond
the pairs of opposites.

Self inflicted pain is not the door to Liberation, but if pain comes, accept it. Live out your karma.

After dead wood is cut out, the tree will flower again.

Karma is a lesson in learning, not punishment.

Spiritual birth can be painful. You are breaking away from worldly life.

It is not in the cosmic plan that we suffer. Most suffering is of our own making.

The Buddha

taught that the lotus grows in water, rooted in mud, but not stained by it. Realize this truth. It is a reward for suffering.

Many physical ailments are based on lack of gratitude. Be grateful for what you have. If you feel depressed, make a list of things to be grateful for.

We can identify with and glorify suffering. This is a self-glorification which is difficult to let go of. It becomes martyrdom.

Self-pity is a thorn in the flesh that in time festers into a wound.

Many people have no will power, only a lot of self will.
That is the source of much self-created pain.

Resentment and that which is resented are on the same chain.

When you hold someone on a chain by your grudges and
criticism, remember that you are on the other end.

The dark night of the soul is for the weakening of
self-will, thereby making the soul receptive.

Survive
**in the eyes of God, that is the only important
thing. Don't compare, don't compete, for that
is self-created pain.**

Competition's true meaning is to win. To win you must fight.
Fighting leads to killing. The root of killing is to compete to win.

Thoughtlessly we develop bad habits and allow them to remain.
Then we cry when we experience the pain of our carelessness.

When we achieve control over a great weakness, the power that was locked up in that weakness is now available to manifest according to our decision.

Co-operate with your course of evolution. Life becomes painful when you fight and manifest your will.

Assume you have volitional power over yourself and circumstances. Act as though you do! Assert this power. "Acting as if" will help you over a hurdle. Circumstances will change.

Enlightenment
is the process of detachment. It is not necessary that we live in pain and suffering.

Mind and Imagination

Yoga means liberation.

We want to free ourselves from limitations now accepted.

The mind is a computer. What are you putting into your computer? Discriminate. Decide what to accept or reject

A new thought is like soft clay. It can be re-shaped. An old thought that has been fired in the kiln of emotions has to be broken with a sledge hammer.

Mind is like a stage.
Personality aspects move around, obeying the dictates of a director.

Names and forms are only for the convenience of the human mind.

Fears are the greatest consumers of your energy. All your fears begin in your mind.

Mental and physical discipline is needed. A drifting mind is the first step to deterioration.

In order to listen to someone you have to stop your own mind. When listening, you are not scheming your own self-gratification.

Tell your body what to do and it will comply. It needs quietening before it can take instruction.

Do not give power to negative thoughts or that is what will manifest.

Reflect before you meditate.
Sit and watch your mind. Deal with what comes up. If you meditate too soon, the subconscious wells up and can be overpowering.

The mind is the vehicle for letting the Creative Force express itself.

Consciousness is the vehicle of Light, the brain is the vehicle of consciousness.

Do not try to make your mind a blank in meditation and concentration. A blank mind is available to anyone who wants it.

Mind the interpreter is a very tricky thing. We hear only what we want to hear.

If you compensate on a physical level, for example, go to a beauty shop — look at this as being symbolic on other levels.

What is the reflection on a perfectly clear mind? The Higher Mind is reflected.

Mind interprets in view of past experience. It is at a loss when new happenings take place. It will try to manoeuvre a situation so it can fit into preconceived ideas.

Character building purifies the mind.

Mind does not die. Mind is part of the consciousness that lives.

Many people suffer from undirected, uncultivated minds. A diamond will only reflect the light when it is cut and polished.

Be non-defensive. What is there to defend and what does it matter?

Imagination
has countless building stones. They must be put together for purposes of accomplishment.

When cleaning or washing dishes, find out what it means symbolically. What aspects of myself am I cleaning up?

The need to believe something often interferes with one's reasoning. A person has the tendency to believe what he wants to.

Observation is a helpful tool to get rid of preconceived ideas or beliefs.

The eyes see — mind is the interpreter.

Learn that you don't have to associate what you experience with something in the past. Just take each experience in itself, for itself.

The wishes and desires you have had in the past are like seeds you have sown. If you don't want them now, ask to have them taken back. Ask in return only for Divine Love.

The five senses, five windows to the world. To perceive — what?

Pre-conceived ideas keep out truth.

Freedom from concepts allows new experience.

Self-mastery is the gateway to liberation.

Confusion
can be a very good thing. It takes away the security that we have all the answers in our pocket.

When stubbornness is directed it becomes will-power and that will help you to get to your goal.

There is power in choice. You can always choose between helping somebody or being critical. That is your choice.

The power of choice is always yours.

The Power

that created

the eye

can see~

Light
on the
Path

In the Divine Light
you are re-affirming your identification.

Dedication and choice destroy obstacles.

Consciousness is a vortex of energy. Many vortexes of energy surround the earth. Be careful what you open yourself to.

You can only learn by making mistakes. Learn from your mistakes. Don't repeat them. Also, learn from the mistakes of others.

Be clear what you know and what you intellectualize. Use discrimination. When you intellectualize, you pretend to yourself that you know. However, true knowing leads to action.

Do not give precious insights to people who are living on a material level. Be an inspiration to others without telling too much.

It is best not to waste time on questions which cannot be answered.

Keep your bliss to yourself.

God doesn't work for you. The Cosmic Force works through you.

Change your attitude
to "I want to do this. I am doing this by choice."

A situation is an opportunity to grow. Respond positively and the situation will change. Once a lesson is learned it no longer repeats.

The hang-up of Christianity is that Jesus will do it for you.
No, you do it for yourself.

Clean out the garbage and God comes in His own time.

The Guru helps you to remove those beliefs that
are as yet untested.

What are you attracted to? What do you like? That is
where you are at.

Approach work
as a master, rather than a slave.

In order to attract higher states, you need a high degree
of surrender. You must surrender thinking, criticism
and judgement of your Guru in order to attract him.

You must take responsibility for whatever manifests in your life.

Ignorance demands trust and faith;
knowledge demands responsibility.

Ignorance is no protection — but innocence.

Ignorance is burned in the fire of wisdom.

If you accept the idea of a spiritual life, or a Supreme Consciousness, it is necessary to develop faith in order to get rid of any feeling of insecurity. To do that, you must turn to that Intelligence or Consciousness.

Wherever you seek the Most High, there you can trust and feel at home.

There is never any time in your life with the final answer, but there is an answer and that is good enough for today.

When in a depressed state, write in the sky with your imagination the word LIGHT. Direct the mind away from the negative up to the Light.

The only permanence is change. Taking change in stride speaks of high development.

Death — going through the other door.

In the course of spiritual growth all of your concepts, ideas and beliefs have to be investigated and re-evaluated over and over again.

An ideal is anything an action is motivated by.

You can change or control the effects of any event past, present or future, if you change your attitude towards that event.

You create your future existence NOW.

All moral sense
should come from your own inner being, your own beliefs.

Poetry on the highest level is often prophetic and ahead of its time.

Art is greatest when dedicated to a higher force.

An artist should surrender to movement, surrender sight to color, and keep out the desire to express self-will. When self is kept out the hand will move.

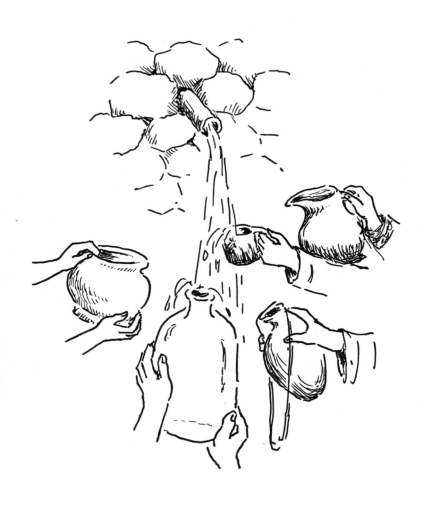

There is only one truth.
There appear to be many truths because of different understandings.

Renunciation

is one way to become free of the
compelling attractions to which the senses
are exposed. It does not mean giving up
joy and happiness.

Fun is gratification of greedy emotions, which are never
satisfied for long anyway. When we pursue joy and inner
happiness, we see the inner beauty of life.

Knowledge not applied is sin.

You can bring quality into the smallest act of your life.

A person of superior intellect is a person who can learn from the
mistakes of others, not having to make them himself.

Life has to become difficult or meaningless before we
begin to think.

Alchemists transformed lead into gold. They raised lower
forces to higher.

Psychic energy is the power of the soul.

The yogi who gives up sex is not moralizing. He is learning
how to use energy.

**"Take time to be holy" means
take time to think.**

Man is a bridge

between two worlds — the bridge is the rainbow
from our world to the spiritual world. Walk across,
taking one step at a time.

You can learn by loving obedience or by force.
Decide which!

The closer you come to God in your consciousness,
the freer you are.

Intense desire creates manifestation.

Be very careful what you read, think, or say before going to
sleep. It always goes into the unconscious. The last thing you
should do before sleep is surround yourself and your bed
with Light.

The more aware you are the less you can be brainwashed.

Attention is power.
**Do not direct it toward too many activities. Clarify
your emotional reaction, then eliminate
as much as possible.**

Get in touch with that which is "dreaming up" this life.
You will then be in touch with your innermost being.

Greediness in the search of the Divine is an ego trip.

Talking about "Oneness" and demonstrating it in life are
two different things.

Think about reincarnation only according to space and time. Beyond space and time in your present concept, there is no reincarnation. Instead of seeing your life in compartments, see it in a flow. Each day in a life is comparable to a lifetime. Each night is comparable to not being incarnated. Or think of each minute on a clock as one lifetime. See yourself in the total of all past existences.

See reincarnation as a tree, one central core sending off branches. Different branches incarnate.

Human relationships are usually thought of in terms of personality. Build a ladder from this ordinary self to the Higher Self. The individual who maintains true calmness and poise, when those around him are losing theirs, is acting from his Higher Self. When negative aspects are manifesting, the lower self has taken over.

Yoga teaches

refinement of the senses. The inner ear is as important as the third eye.

Deify with discrimination. You can make your own heart the tabernacle of that which you want to worship.

God is a big trickster. If he doesn't get you one way, he gets you another.

Your own soul, gateway to the Highest within yourself, will get information and give it to you through dreams.

Don't defend yourself. That is all ego.

Do not strive. There is no need to strive. Just relax and Be.

God comes in his own time. His presence cannot be commanded.

There should always be a proper balance of doing and wanting to do.

Who has the authority to judge? I cannot judge because what I think is right or wrong is based on my own personal ideas, my social level, and the culture in which I was born.

Religions

can be different, but the ideals the same.
All can move in the same way toward the goal
of the Most High.

By making religious differences and emphasizing them,
we give ourselves self-importance.

Doctrines are man-made. God's voice can be heard
in the stillness of your inner being.

The Higher Self is the gateway between
ordinary consciousness and God.

Spiritual practice leads to de-hypnotising and
reconditioning ourselves.

Attain the power to create and destroy worlds. Destroy your old concepts! Build a new world by forming your own concepts, without attachments. Keep free, suspended. Make your bridge from this world to the spiritual world a suspension bridge.

Oneness is beyond sense perception.

Obedience is surrendering your will.

When you give up your will, there is perfect harmony.

Yoga is a path of liberation. Liberate yourself from your cherished convictions, become your own opponent.

The seed

already contains the oak. In the embryo the genius is already forming.

Toward
Awareness

Turn to your innermost being. Even God does not enter your mind without your permission.

There is a body-mind, like a computer with emotions. It is very teachable. What are you teaching it? To be well? To be sick? To be over-sensitive?

What is perfection?

You don't know; you only have your concepts.
Perfect surrender to Divine Will is the only perfection.

Perfection cannot manifest on the human level.

Between two actions in life, between two tragedies, there is a moment to recuperate. "Between two breaths, realize."

Life forces us into surrender. The less we struggle to have our own will, the easier it will be.

Some thoughts are like weeds. Some are like flowers.

To be rooted in the earth is to be part of the cycle of flowers and fruit. To be uprooted takes strength. To be rooted in heaven one has to overcome.

Think of yourself as a flower becoming open to
Divine love. This is symbolic mentally and emotionally.

Divine Light
has no qualities. All qualities are human.

Only false pride is harmful. Be proud of your accomplishments.

Whatever life's experiences are, surrender to them; face them.
A lesson once learned will never be repeated.

The life you live is a dream, intermingling with
the dreams of others.

Like a cook who cleans the pot before cooking a new meal,
clean out your mind in preparation for new thoughts
and experiences.

The first stage of samadhi will not take place until you have
overcome selfish desires.

Selfless service will make you Divine.

Ponder each day's happenings. Expand your awareness. Do not intellectualize. Otherwise your life is mechanical. It is like a fruit that is dry and shrivelled up. Watered with awareness, the fruit becomes ripe, juicy, delicious. Daily pondering is watering the fruit of your life.

Have faith.

Support from the Divine doesn't come too soon because it is important for you to grow stronger. This will happen only by your taking your own steps.

Allow yourself time to understand. Don't go racing through your life, but don't get sidetracked either. Find the happy medium.

The only true knowledge comes from personal experience.

In the spiritual quest everything depends on the degree of sincerity and dedication.

We must not confuse excess with quality.

Never use knowledge or emotion as a weapon against others. Never stir up anyone's imagination for your benefit.

Total renunciation means giving up emotional attachments to material things, then emotional attachments to cherished ideas and beliefs.

Control of emotions, increased awareness, loss of fear, growing courage, an inner knowing and security all pave the road to Self-realization and give proof to the aspirant that the Road is indeed real.

Reflection leads to control of the ideas arising in the mind.

Those potentials that have been developed to an unusual degree by a few human beings were brought about by constant searching, never taking anything for granted, never accepting any limit. Limits are an end.

Guru — a teacher. An ant teaching persistence.

Learning is a process of trial and error. Error is not sin.

Sin is acting against one's better knowledge.

The key

to the whole process is two-fold. Concentration and awareness. Together these produce intuition which is awareness to the highest degree.

What we can learn from the East is the ability to listen with intuition, to think with intuition and to bring intuition into the foreground so that it becomes a reliable tool. That is the training which is missed in the West.

Know the difference between intuition and emotion. The inner command of intuition is beyond emotion.

Intuition can be looked upon as a Gateway to a new dimension.

When you keep judgement suspended, then the intuition comes in.

Saraswati

Intuition
is the fruit of contemplation.

All spiritual practice

is reprogramming yourself until you reach a state
of awareness where you can forget about
programming.

Awareness is the vital ingredient for all personal development.

To become aware and to know yourself is the Path that
leads to freedom.

**Awareness is your special gift.
Be grateful for it.**

Humility

is the number one trait for embarking on the spiritual life.

As you inquire about Higher Knowledge, it will come to you.

Fear blocks. Faith removes the obstacle of fear.

What is hope? It is part of the survival kit. It keeps you moving and can keep you running forever.

Cut out anxiety by surrendering to the situation.

Anxiety can be traced to an uncultivated imagination.

An uncultivated ear does not hear. An uncultivated mind cannot know.

Unless the mind is truly empty of all concepts about who you are, and the resulting self-importance, nothing much is going to happen.

Sense perceptions and emotional reactions hold us prisoners.

Besides the intellect, the emotions also have to be cultivated. Humility is the most neglected emotion.

Always doubt for the sake of knowing more. Knowing more means greater responsibility.

Your own sincerity in the search is your best protection.

Sincerity is the guiding Light.

Mantra of the
Divine Light Invocation

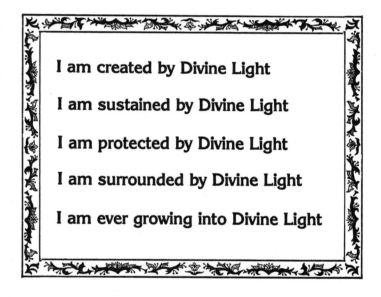

I am created by Divine Light

I am sustained by Divine Light

I am protected by Divine Light

I am surrounded by Divine Light

I am ever growing into Divine Light